AMERICAN DOCUMENTS

The Emancipation Proclamation

Union soldier

Marianne McComb

Picture Credits

Cover (flag), cover (Lincoln) Getty Images; cover (document), 7, 10 courtesy the Library of Congress; page 1 Minnesota Historical Society/Corbis; pages 2-3 Kevin Fleming/Corbis; pages 4, 4-5, 11 (bottom) 16-17, 19, 20-21, 22, 25, 28, 29 Bettmann/Corbis; page 6 Lester Lefkowitz/Corbis; page 8 Art Resource, NY; page 9 Hulton Archive/Getty Images; pages 11 (top), 14-15 The Corcoran Gallery of Art/Corbis; pages 12, 16, 23, 24 (bottom), 26, 31 Corbis; page 13 Bob Krist/Corbis; page 18 The Granger Collection, NY; page 24 (top) Todd A. Gipstein/Corbis; page 27 Christie's Images/Corbis; page 30 Larry Downing/Corbis Sygma.

Produced through the worldwide resources of the National Geographic Society, John M. Fahey, Jr., President and Chief Executive Officer; Gilbert M. Grosvenor, Chairman of the Board; Nina D. Hoffman, Executive Vice President and President, Books and Education Publishing Group.

Prepared by National Geographic School Publishing and Children's Books

Ericka Markman, Senior Vice President and President, Children's Books and Education Publishing Group; Steve Mico, Vice President, Editorial Director; Marianne Hiland, Executive Editor; Anita Schwartz, Project Editor; Suzanne Patrick Fonda, Children's Books Project Editor; Jim Hiscott, Design Manager; Kristin Hanneman, Illustrations Manager; Diana Bourdrez, Picture Editor; Matt Wascavage, Manager of Publishing Services; Sean Philpotts, Production Manager.

Manufacturing and Quality Management

Christopher A. Liedel, Chief Financial Officer; Phillip L. Schlosser, Director; Clifton M. Brown III, Manager.

Art Direction

Dan Banks, Project Design Company

Consultants/Reviewers

Dr. Paul Finkelman, Chapman Distinguished Professor of Law, University of Tulsa Law School, Tulsa, Oklahoma

Dr. Margit E. McGuire, School of Education, Seattle University, Seattle, Washington

Book Development

Nieman Inc.

Book Design

Steven Curtis Design, Inc.

Photo Research

Corrine L. Brock, In the Lupe, Inc.

ISBN: 0-7922-7916-6 (hardcover)
ISBN: 0-7922-7936-0 (library)

Library of Congress CIP data available on request

Previously published as *Documents of Freedom: The Emancipation Proclamation* (National Geographic Reading Expeditions), copyright © 2004; ISBN: 0-7922-4555-5 (paperback)

Published by the National Geographic Society
1145 17th Street, N.W.
Washington, D.C. 20036-4688

Printed in the U.S.A.

Table of Contents

The Lincoln Memorial, Washington Monument, and Capitol lit by fireworks

Introduction

What if slavery still existed in the United States? What if human beings could be bought and sold like pieces of furniture? How different would our country be? Would we even have a country? African slavery existed in America for over 200 years. It divided Americans as no other issue in our history ever has. Slavery caused a long, bitter struggle between some Americans who wanted to keep it and others who wanted to stop it. In the end, Americans had to fight one another in the Civil War before slavery was banned in the United States.

Slavery was a major cause of the Civil War.

In the middle of that war, President Abraham Lincoln issued the Emancipation Proclamation. *Emancipate* means "free from slavery." The Emancipation Proclamation was a major step in the long struggle to end slavery in the United States.

Why did slavery exist in the United States? Why did some Americans want to keep it and some want to end it? Why did Lincoln issue the Emancipation Proclamation when he did? What did the document mean? What effects did it have on later events? Let's find out.

At slave auctions, human beings were bought and sold.

On Display

In 1936, the official copy of the Emancipation Proclamation was placed in the National Archives in Washington, D.C. Over the years, the document has been put on public display several times.

Lincoln's Draft

The original draft of the Emancipation Proclamation was mostly handwritten by President Abraham Lincoln. This document was later donated to a home for disabled soldiers in Chicago. The original was destroyed in the Chicago fire of 1871.

Official Copy

The official copy of the Emancipation Proclamation was written by a government clerk in ink on five sheets of paper. These were tied together with narrow red and blue ribbons.

Who Signed?

The official document was signed by President Abraham Lincoln and by Secretary of State William H. Seward.

...all persons held as slaves within any State or designated part of a State, the people whereof shall then be in rebellion against the United States, shall be then, thenceforward, and forever free...

By the President of the United States of America:

A Proclamation.

Whereas, on the twenty-second day of September, in the year of our Lord one thousand eight hundred and sixty-two, a proclamation was issued by the President of the United States, containing, among other things, the following, to wit:

"That on the first day of January, in the
"year of our Lord one thousand eight hundred
"and sixty-three, all persons held as slaves within
"any State or designated part of a State, the people
"whereof shall then be in rebellion against the
"United States, shall be then, thenceforward, and
"forever free; and the Executive Government of the
"United States, including the military and naval
"authority thereof, will recognize and maintain
"the freedom of such persons, and will do no act
"or acts to repress such persons, or any of them,
"in any efforts they may make for their actual
"freedom.
    "That the Executive will, on the first day

7

The Road to War

The Civil War came about because people in two parts of our country—the North and the South—lived very different lives.

★

A Country Divided

During the early 1800s, the northern and southern parts of the United States became very different societies. Many Northerners were farmers, but the farms were small. There were also many factories and large cities in the North.

Life in the South was different. Unlike the North, the South had few large cities and factories. Southern farms were often very large. These large farms, called **plantations,** needed the help of many workers. Slaves had been brought from Africa to work on southern plantations until this trade was outlawed in 1808. By then, nearly one million slaves lived in the United States.

Slavery never became an important part of life in the North. Although some Northerners did own slaves, most did not. In the South, however, slavery was vital to the economy.

Slaves work on a Mississippi cotton plantation.

In 1837, a pro-slavery mob burned the office of an abolitionist newspaper in Illinois and killed its editor, Elijah Lovejoy.

Struggle Over Slavery

Many people in the North felt slavery was wrong. Some Northerners acted on their beliefs. They started a movement to stop slavery. They were called **abolitionists** because they wanted to abolish, or end, slavery. In the South, people believed that it was their right to own slaves. They said that the government had no right to tell them what to do with their "property"—meaning their slaves.

To make matters worse, some western territories were asking Congress to become states. Would the new states be slave or free? In 1819, when the territory of Missouri applied to be a state, there was a great debate. The problem was solved when Maine, for years part of Massachusetts, asked to become a separate state. To keep a balance between slave and free states, Congress voted to admit Missouri as a slave state and Maine as a free state. Congress also decided where slavery would be legal in new territories. This agreement was known as the **Missouri Compromise.**

Map from 1856 showing slave states (brown), free states (red), and western territories (green)

Compromise Fails

For a while, the Missouri Compromise kept the peace. When the United States gained the territories of California and New Mexico, the debate heated up again. Another compromise was needed. The **Compromise of 1850** said that California would be a free state. It also said that voters in Utah and New Mexico would decide for themselves whether their states would be slave or free.

The Compromise of 1850 also included a new **Fugitive Slave Law.** Its purpose was to help southern slave owners recapture escaped slaves. Many Northerners were unhappy with this law. Before 1850, slaves who had escaped from the South and made it to the North were usually able to live in freedom. With the new law, these slaves could more easily be hunted down and returned to their masters.

Lincoln Is Elected

The tension between North and South grew even worse with the election of 1860. When a Northerner, Abraham Lincoln of Illinois, was elected President, people in the South were angry and fearful. They knew Lincoln did not want slavery to spread. This meant that the earlier balance between slave and free states would no longer exist.

Lincoln promised that he would not touch slavery where it already existed, but most Southerners did not believe him. Instead, seven states (South Carolina, Georgia, Alabama, Florida, Mississippi, Louisiana, and Texas) voted to secede from—or leave—the United States. Later, North Carolina, Arkansas, Tennessee, and Virginia left as well.

Lincoln told the southern states that *under no condition* could they leave the **Union**. The South ignored him. They formed their own government, the **Confederate States of America.**

Abraham Lincoln

Lincoln saw slavery as a "monstrous injustice." However, he was not an abolitionist. He did not feel that the solution to what he saw as a complex problem was to simply free all the slaves at once.

Lincoln's inauguration in 1861

War Comes

President Lincoln promised that he would defend the United States against the Confederacy. On April 12, 1861, Confederates attacked Fort Sumter in South Carolina. The Civil War had begun.

⭐

Lincoln's Problems

Those first shots fired on Fort Sumter made it clear that there was no avoiding a war between North and South. Was the war about **secession**—leaving the Union—or slavery? This was a big problem for President Lincoln.

Most Northerners believed that the purpose of the war was to reunite the country. Lincoln himself said many times that this was a fight to save the Union. It was *not* a war to end slavery.

The South's attack on Fort Sumter started the Civil War.

Lincoln had a personal dislike for slavery. However, he believed that the Constitution did not allow the federal government to interfere with slavery. He also worried that soldiers in his army would refuse to fight if they thought the war was about slavery.

In the South, people believed the war was about protecting their way of life. They wanted things in the South to continue just as they had in the past. Of course, this meant keeping slavery. Another of Lincoln's problems was to keep loyal those slave states that had *not* left the Union. If the North was seen to be fighting a war to end slavery, **border states** such as Missouri and Kentucky might join the Confederates.

To add to Lincoln's problems, by the summer of 1862, the North seemed to be losing the war. Under able leaders like Robert E. Lee, the Confederates won great victories. Fewer and fewer men volunteered to fight for the Union. Worst of all, the public had begun to question Lincoln's ability to lead.

His victories made Robert E. Lee a hero to Southerners.

Frederick Douglass Speaks Out

Northern abolitionists were angry that Lincoln refused to make the war about slavery. They felt that the war had given him the perfect opportunity to end this evil forever. Because Lincoln refused to take a stand on slavery, they tried to get Congress to pass laws that made it possible for slaves to join the northern war effort. They argued that freed slaves could help the North win the war.

Many people offered the President ideas about how to win the war. One of the strongest and clearest voices was that of Frederick Douglass. He was an escaped slave who had become a well-known speaker and abolitionist leader. Douglass argued to Lincoln that the slavery question was holding the North back from victory. If Lincoln did not abolish slavery, Douglass warned, the South would win the war and the nation would be forever divided.

During the war, the Union armies seized southern property, such as this plantation, which they used as a headquarters.

Douglass's advice to Lincoln was that he make slavery *the* issue of the war. He helped Lincoln see that when people believe in the rightness of their cause, they are willing to fight and die for it. Ending the evil of slavery, Douglass said, was a better cause than preserving the Union.

Lincoln now understood what he should do. Under the Constitution, he had no power to touch slavery. However, as commander in chief of the army, he could take away his enemies' property—including their slaves—in time of war. Lincoln would free only those slaves held in the states at war with the Union. He would encourage these former slaves to enlist in the Union armies. Here was a plan that would hurt the Confederacy, help the Union, and not violate the Constitution.

Frederick Douglass

Frederick Douglass was born into slavery in Maryland in 1818. Twenty years later, he escaped to freedom in the North and became involved in the antislavery movement.

Lincoln Makes a Decision

Lincoln thought about Douglass's advice all through the spring of 1862. Then he began writing. By July, Lincoln was ready to share his ideas with his **cabinet,** or group of chief advisers. Lincoln told them, "Gentleman, it appears that we must change our tactics or lose the game." He explained that they would have to free the slaves to win the war.

Lincoln's announcement shocked his cabinet. They could not believe that he would do such a thing. *Free the slaves?* No President in history had ever taken such a big step. It was the cabinet's job to support the President and his policies. So, they listened as Lincoln read aloud a rough draft of his Emancipation Proclamation.

Lincoln's closest adviser, Secretary of State William H. Seward, said freeing the slaves was a good idea. He also thought that the President should wait to make his announcement until after the northern army won an important battle. Otherwise, people might think that Lincoln was freeing the slaves out of desperation. The President agreed.

William H. Seward

William H. Seward of New York was a leader of the antislavery movement. He opposed the Compromise of 1850 and the Fugitive Slave Law. After Lincoln was elected President in 1860, Seward became his Secretary of State and one of his closest advisers.

Two months later, the Confederate army invaded Maryland. On September 17, about 24,000 Union and Confederate soldiers were killed or wounded at the battle of Antietam. Afterwards, the Confederates retreated back into Virginia. Lincoln had the victory he was waiting for. On September 22, 1862, the President read the Emancipation Proclamation to the public for the first time. He told the country it would go into effect in 100 days (January 1, 1863).

Lincoln reads the Emancipation Proclamation to his cabinet. William Seward is seated in front of the table.

A Closer Look

The Emancipation Proclamation reads like a legal contract, something you would hear in a courtroom. It is filled with words like whereof, thenceforward, *and* aforesaid. *What did it mean?*

★

Who Was Freed?

It is important to be clear about what the Emancipation Proclamation did *not* mean. It did not end slavery. What the Emancipation Proclamation did was free all slaves living in a state that was rebelling against the United States. This meant Arkansas, Texas, Mississippi, Alabama, Florida, Georgia, South Carolina, North Carolina, and parts of Louisiana and Virginia. The Emancipation Proclamation did not free slaves in states that had not joined the Confederates—Maryland, Delaware, Kentucky, and Missouri. It also did not free slaves in parts of the South that were now back under Union control, such as Tennessee and West Virginia.

Fleeing to the Union lines in 1862, these runaway slaves crossed a river in Virginia.

Why Didn't Lincoln End Slavery?

The answer to this question lies in understanding Lincoln as a leader and as a person. As President, Lincoln's most important goal was to win the war and restore the Union. He worried that freeing slaves in states that were loyal to the Union might cause these states to secede.

As a person, Lincoln clearly believed that slavery was wrong. As a lawyer, he understood the Constitution limited his power to end slavery. Lincoln wrote, "I am naturally antislavery. If slavery is not wrong, nothing is wrong. I cannot remember when I did not so think and feel. And yet I never understood that the Presidency conferred upon me an unrestricted right to act officially upon this judgment and feeling."

"abstain from all violence... labor faithfully for reasonable wages"

Lincoln forbade the freed slaves from using violence against their former masters, except in self-defense. He also urged them to remain with their masters and work for fair wages.

Lincoln visited the Union camp at Antietam a few weeks after the battle.

North and South React

Many Northerners praised Lincoln for his decision to free the slaves. However, some abolitionists attacked him for not going far enough. They argued that the President should have taken this opportunity to end slavery in *all* parts of the country.

Southerners were outraged by the Emancipation Proclamation. They accused the President of trying to start a slave revolt. This had always been one of the South's worst fears.

African-American soldiers of the Union army

They also were angered by Lincoln's attempt to take away what they saw as their property. Southerners vowed they would release no slaves unless the Union army marched in and forced them to do so.

Fortunately, many southern slaves decided to take matters into their own hands. Rather than wait for their freedom, these slaves escaped to the protection of nearby Union army camps. As Lincoln had hoped, thousands of former slaves decided to enlist and fight for the Union. There were nearly 200,000 black soldiers and sailors before the war was over. Twenty-three were awarded the Medal of Honor, the nation's highest military award.

"persons of suitable condition, will be received into the armed service of the United States"

Lincoln invited all freed male slaves to enlist and help win the war. Both sides saw this as critical. A Confederate admitted, "If slaves will make good soldiers, our whole theory of slavery is wrong."

A New Birth of Freedom

The Emancipation Proclamation became official on January 1, 1863. Terrible fighting continued in the months that followed.

★

The Battle of Gettysburg

Once again, Confederate forces invaded the North. On July 1, they met the Union army near Gettysburg, Pennsylvania. Over the next three days, the two sides fought the greatest battle of the war.

Pickett's Charge at the battle of Gettysburg

The first two days ended with neither side in control. On the third day, Confederate commander Robert E. Lee took a huge risk. He ordered 15,000 Confederates under the command of General George Pickett to charge the center of the Union army. Pickett's Charge failed to break the Union lines. Only half of the Confederates made it back. The next day, Lee ordered a retreat. Gettysburg was a major victory for the North. It marked a turning point in the war.

In November, a cemetery for the Union soldiers who died at Gettysburg was going to be dedicated. President Lincoln was invited to say a few words at the dedication ceremony. In this speech, now known as the Gettysburg Address, Lincoln revealed that he had changed his mind about the purpose of the war. The speech also made clear his dedication to equality.

Confederate dead at Gettysburg gathered for burial

23

An End to Slavery

The battle of Gettysburg was the turning point of the Civil War.

★

Surrender at Appomattox

Shortly after Lincoln gave his Gettysburg Address, the Union army began a destructive march south across Georgia and north through the Carolinas. By April 1865, the Confederacy's hopes of winning the war had ended.

The Civil War left much of the South in ruins.

On April 9, Confederate commander Robert E. Lee surrendered to Union commander Ulysses S. Grant. That very day, Lincoln began planning how to bring the Confederacy back into the Union. He wanted to begin to heal the nation's wounds as quickly as possible.

Tragically, Lincoln would never see his plans carried through. Five days after the surrender at Appomattox, Lincoln was shot while he and his wife were at a theater in Washington, D.C. He died the next day. Across the country and around the world, people mourned the death of a great leader.

Two months after Lincoln's death, Major General Gordon Granger of the Union army led his troops into the city of Galveston, Texas. On June 19, 1865, Granger officially proclaimed freedom for all slaves in Texas. The freed slaves gathered in celebration. Thousands of people jammed the streets of Galveston. There was singing, dancing, and weeping as the men, women, and children rejoiced in their freedom. To this day, the event, called **Juneteenth,** is celebrated in various parts of the United States.

Former slaves hear the news of the Emancipation Proclamation.

Civil Rights Amendments

True freedom and equality for African Americans would be terribly slow in coming. Shortly before Lincoln's death, Congress passed the Thirteenth Amendment to the Constitution. This amendment made slavery illegal in the United States and all its territories. It became law in December 1865.

These freed African Americans were living in a southern town shortly after the Civil War.

African Americans vote for the first time following the passage of the Fifteenth Amendment.

The Thirteenth Amendment was not enough. In the South, newly freed slaves were being denied their rights of American citizenship. For example, they were not permitted to vote or hold public office. They were not allowed to live where they wanted to live. They were not permitted to educate their children the way they wanted to educate them. In 1868, Congress took action again. The Fourteenth Amendment was meant to guarantee that all American citizens, no matter what their color, were entitled to all the rights of U.S. citizens.

Two years later, Congress was forced to step in once again. Southern states were preventing African Americans from voting. The Fifteenth Amendment said that no citizens could be kept from voting because of their color or because they were once slaves.

A Long Struggle

Lincoln understood the importance of the Emancipation Proclamation. "If I go down in history," he predicted, "it will be for this act." However, African Americans had to struggle for their rights long after the Civil War ended slavery. Beginning in the late 1800s, southern states passed many laws to maintain **segregation,** or the separation of people by race. These laws forced African Americans to use separate, and generally inferior, public and private facilities than those used by whites. Not until the civil rights movement of the 1950s and 1960s, was segregation made illegal. In the years since then, African Americans have made huge strides toward the full equality envisioned by Abraham Lincoln in the Gettysburg Address.

On October 16, 1995, the Million Man March in Washington, D.C., renewed a commitment by African Americans to full equality.

Glossary

abolitionist a person who wanted to abolish, or end, slavery

border states slave states, such as Missouri and Kentucky, that did not secede from the Union at the time of the Civil War

cabinet chief advisers to the U.S. President

Compromise of 1850 a series of laws that admitted California as a free state, left the question of slavery in the new territories of the West to be decided by their people, and promised a stronger law to help slave owners recapture runaway slaves

Confederate States of America the 11 southern states that left the United States in 1860 and 1861

Fugitive Slave Law the 1850 law that encouraged the capture of runaway slaves by punishing people who helped them

Juneteenth a holiday observing the announcement of the Emancipation Proclamation in Texas on June 19, 1865

Missouri Compromise a series of laws passed in 1820 to keep the balance between slave states and free states in the Union

plantation a large farm on which crops are raised, often by workers who live on the plantation

secession the act of leaving the Union

segregation separation of people, often by race

Union the United States of America during the Civil War

Drummer boy in an African-American regiment during the Civil War

The Fugitive Slave Act, 1850

Sections 5–10

These sections describe the duties of the courts and law enforcement, the rights of slaveowners, and the penalties for not abiding by the provisions of the act.

To see the complete document, go to the Avalon Project at Yale Law School: www.yale.edu/lawweb/avalon/fugitive.htm

Section 5

And be it further enacted, That it shall be the duty of all marshals and deputy marshals to obey and execute all warrants and precepts issued under the provisions of this act, when to them directed; and should any marshal or deputy marshal refuse to receive such warrant, or other process, when tendered, or to use all proper means diligently to execute the same, he shall, on conviction thereof, be fined in the sum of one thousand dollars, to the use of such claimant, on the motion of such claimant, by the Circuit or District Court for the district of such marshal; and after arrest of such fugitive, by such marshal or his deputy, or whilst at any time in his custody under the provisions of this act, should such fugitive escape, whether with or without the assent of such marshal or his deputy, such marshal shall be liable, on his official bond, to be prosecuted for the benefit of such claimant, for the full value of the service or labor of said fugitive in the State, Territory, or District whence he escaped: and the better to enable the said commissioners, when thus appointed, to execute their duties faithfully and efficiently, in conformity with the requirements of the Constitution of the United States and of this act, they are hereby authorized and empowered, within their counties respectively, to appoint, in writing under their hands, any one or more suitable persons, from time to time, to execute all such warrants and other process as may be issued by them in the lawful performance of their respective duties; with authority to such commissioners, or the persons to be appointed by them, to execute process as aforesaid, to summon and call to their aid the bystanders, or posse comitatus of the proper county, when necessary to ensure a faithful observance of the clause of the Constitution referred to, in conformity with the provisions of this act; and all good citizens are hereby commanded to aid and assist in the prompt and efficient execution of this law, whenever their services may be required, as aforesaid, for that purpose; and said warrants shall run, and be executed by said officers, any where in the State within which they are issued.

Section 6

And be it further enacted, That when a person held to service or labor in any State or Territory of the United States, has heretofore or shall hereafter escape into another State or Territory of the United States, the person or persons to whom such service or labor may be due, or his, her, or their agent or attorney, duly authorized, by power of attorney, in writing, acknowledged and certified under the seal of some legal officer or court of the State or Territory in which the same may be executed, may pursue and reclaim such fugitive person, either by procuring a warrant from some one of the courts, judges, or commissioners aforesaid, of the proper circuit, district, or county, for the apprehension of such fugitive from service or labor, or by seizing and arresting such fugitive, where the same can be done without process, and by taking, or causing such person to be taken, forthwith before such court, judge, or commissioner, whose duty it shall be to hear and determine the case of such claimant in a summary manner; and upon satisfactory proof being made, by deposition or affidavit, in writing, to be taken and certified by such court, judge, or commissioner, or by other satisfactory testimony, duly taken and certified by some court, magistrate, justice of the peace, or other legal officer authorized to administer an oath and take depositions under the laws of the State or Territory from which such person owing service or labor may have escaped, with a certificate of such magistracy or other authority, as aforesaid, with the seal of the proper court or officer thereto attached, which seal shall be sufficient to establish the competency of the proof, and with proof, also by affidavit, of the identity of the person whose service or labor is claimed to be due as aforesaid, that the person so arrested does in fact owe service or labor to the person or persons claiming him or her, in the State or Territory from which such fugitive may have escaped as aforesaid, and that said person escaped, to make out and deliver to such claimant, his or her agent or attorney, a certificate setting forth the substantial facts as to the service or labor due from such fugitive to the claimant, and of his or her escape from the State or Territory in which he or she was arrested, with authority to such claimant, or his or her agent or attorney, to use such reasonable force and restraint as may be necessary, under the circumstances of the case, to take and remove such fugitive person back to the State or Territory whence he or she may have escaped as aforesaid. In no trial or hearing under this act shall the testimony of such alleged fugitive be admitted in evidence; and the certificates in this and the first [fourth] section mentioned, shall be conclusive of the right of the person or persons in whose favor granted, to remove such fugitive to the State or Territory from which he escaped, and shall prevent all molestation of such person or persons by any process issued by any court, judge, magistrate, or other person whomsoever.

Section 7

And be it further enacted, That any person who shall knowingly and willingly obstruct, hinder, or prevent such claimant, his agent or attorney, or any person or persons lawfully assisting him, her, or them, from arresting such a fugitive from service or labor, either with or without process as aforesaid, or shall rescue, or attempt to rescue, such fugitive from service or labor, from the custody of such claimant, his or her agent or attorney, or other person or persons lawfully assisting as aforesaid, when so arrested, pursuant to the authority herein given and declared; or shall aid, abet, or assist such person so owing service or labor as aforesaid, directly or indirectly, to escape from such claimant, his agent or attorney, or other person or persons legally authorized as aforesaid; or shall harbor or conceal such fugitive, so as to prevent the discovery and arrest of such person, after notice or knowledge of the fact that such person was a fugitive from service or labor as aforesaid, shall, for either of said offences, be subject to a fine not exceeding one thousand dollars, and imprisonment not exceeding six months, by indictment and conviction before the District Court of the United States for the district in which such offence may have been committed, or before the proper court of criminal jurisdiction, if committed within any one of the organized Territories of the United States; and shall moreover forfeit and pay, by way of civil damages to the party injured by such illegal conduct, the sum of one thousand dollars for each fugitive so lost as aforesaid, to be recovered by action of debt, in any of the District or Territorial Courts aforesaid, within whose jurisdiction the said offence may have been committed.

Section 8

And be it further enacted, That the marshals, their deputies, and the clerks of the said District and Territorial Courts, shall be paid, for their services, the like fees as may be allowed for similar services in other cases; and where such services are rendered exclusively in the arrest, custody, and delivery of the fugitive to the claimant, his or her agent or attorney, or where such supposed fugitive may be discharged out of custody for the want of sufficient proof as aforesaid, then such fees are to be paid in whole by such claimant, his or her agent or attorney; and in all cases where the proceedings are before a commissioner, he shall be entitled to a fee of ten dollars in full for his services in each case, upon the delivery of the said certificate to the claimant, his agent or attorney; or a fee of five dollars in cases where the proof shall not, in the opinion of such commissioner, warrant such certificate and delivery, inclusive of all services incident to such arrest and examination, to be paid, in either case, by the claimant, his or her agent or attorney. The person or persons authorized to execute the process to be issued by such commissioner for the arrest and detention of fugitives from service or labor as aforesaid, shall also be entitled to a fee of five dollars each for each person he or they may arrest, and take before any commissioner as aforesaid, at the instance and request of such claimant, with such other fees as may be deemed reasonable by such commissioner for such other additional services as may be necessarily performed by him or them; such as attending at the examination, keeping the fugitive in custody, and providing him with food and lodging during his detention, and until the final determination of such commissioners; and, in general, for performing such other duties as may be required by such claimant, his or her attorney or agent, or commissioner in the premises, such fees to be made up in conformity with the fees usually charged by the officers of the courts of justice within the proper district or county, as near as may be practicable, and paid by such claimants, their agents or attorneys, whether such supposed fugitives from service or labor be ordered to be delivered to such claimant by the final determination of such commissioner or not.

Section 9

And be it further enacted, That, upon affidavit made by the claimant of such fugitive, his agent or attorney, after such certificate has been issued, that he has reason to apprehend that such fugitive will he rescued by force from his or their possession before he can be taken beyond the limits of the State in which the arrest is made, it shall be the duty of the officer making the arrest to retain such fugitive in his custody, and to remove him to the State whence he fled, and there to deliver him to said claimant, his agent, or attorney. And to this end, the officer aforesaid is hereby authorized and required to employ so many persons as he may deem necessary to overcome such force, and to retain them in his service so long as circumstances may require. The said officer and his assistants, while so employed, to receive the same compensation, and to be allowed the same expenses, as are now allowed by law for transportation of criminals, to be certified by the judge of the district within which the arrest is made, and paid out of the treasury of the United States.

Section 10

And be it further enacted, That when any person held to service or labor in any State or Territory, or in the District of Columbia, shall escape therefrom, the party to whom such service or labor shall be due, his, her, or their agent or attorney, may apply to any court of record therein, or judge thereof in vacation, and make satisfactory proof to such court, or judge in vacation, of the escape aforesaid, and that the person escaping owed service or labor to such party. Whereupon the court shall cause a record to be made of the matters so proved, and also a general description of the person so escaping, with such convenient certainty as may be; and a transcript of such record, authenticated by the attestation of the clerk and of the seal of the said court, being produced in any other State, Territory, or district in which the person so escaping may be found, and being exhibited to any judge, commissioner, or other office, authorized by the law of the United States to cause persons escaping from service or labor to be delivered up, shall be held and taken to be full and conclusive evidence of the fact of escape, and that the service or labor of the person escaping is due to the party in such record mentioned. And upon the production by the said party of other and further evidence if necessary, either oral or by affidavit, in addition to what is contained in the said record of the identity of the person escaping, he or she shall be delivered up to the claimant, And the said court, commissioner, judge, or other person authorized by this act to grant certificates to claimants or fugitives, shall, upon the production of the record and other evidences aforesaid, grant to such claimant a certificate of his right to take any such person identified and proved to be owing service or labor as aforesaid, which certificate shall authorize such claimant to seize or arrest and transport such person to the State or Territory from which he escaped: Provided, That nothing herein contained shall be construed as requiring the production of a transcript of such record as evidence as aforesaid. But in its absence the claim shall be heard and determined upon other satisfactory proofs, competent in law.

Approved, September 18, 1850.

The Emancipation Proclamation

By the President of the
United States of America:

A PROCLAMATION

Whereas on the 22nd day of September, A.D. 1862, a proclamation was issued by the President of the United States, containing, among other things, the following, to wit:

"That on the 1st day of January, A.D. 1863, all persons held as slaves within any State or designated part of a State the people whereof shall then be in rebellion against the United States shall be then, thenceforward, and forever free; and the executive government of the United States, including the military and naval authority thereof, will recognize and maintain the freedom of such persons and will do no act or acts to repress such persons, or any of them, in any efforts they may make for their actual freedom.

"That the executive will on the 1st day of January aforesaid, by proclamation, designate the States and parts of States, if any, in which the people thereof, respectively, shall then be in rebellion against the United States; and the fact that any State or the people thereof shall on that day be in good faith represented in the Congress of the United States by members chosen thereto at elections wherein a majority of the qualified voters of such States shall have participated shall, in the absence of strong countervailing testimony, be deemed conclusive evidence that such State and the people thereof are not then in rebellion against the United States."

Now, therefore, I, Abraham Lincoln, President of the United States, by virtue of the power in me vested as Commander-In-Chief of the Army and Navy of the United States in time of actual armed rebellion against the authority and government of the United States, and as a fit and necessary war measure for supressing said rebellion, do, on this 1st day of January, A.D. 1863, and in accordance with my purpose so to do, publicly proclaimed for the full period of one hundred days from the first day above mentioned, order and designate as the States and parts of States wherein the people thereof, respectively, are this day in rebellion against the United States the following, to wit:

Arkansas, Texas, Louisiana (except the parishes of St. Bernard, Palquemines, Jefferson, St. John, St. Charles, St. James, Ascension, Assumption, Terrebone, Lafourche, St. Mary, St. Martin, and Orleans, including the city of New Orleans), Mississippi, Alabama, Florida, Georgia, South Carolina, North Carolina, and Virginia (except the forty-eight counties designated as West Virginia, and also the counties of Berkeley, Accomac, Morthhampton, Elizabeth City, York, Princess Anne, and Norfolk, including the cities of Norfolk and Portsmouth), and which excepted parts are for the present left precisely as if this proclamation were not issued.

And by virtue of the power and for the purpose aforesaid, I do order and declare that all persons held as slaves within said designated States and parts of States are, and henceforward shall be, free; and that the Executive Government of the United States, including the military and naval authorities thereof, will recognize and maintain the freedom of said persons.

And I hereby enjoin upon the people so declared to be free to abstain from all violence, unless in necessary self-defence; and I recommend to them that, in all case when allowed, they labor faithfully for reasonable wages.

And I further declare and make known that such persons of suitable condition will be received into the armed service of the United States to garrison forts, positions, stations, and other places, and to man vessels of all sorts in said service.

And upon this act, sincerely believed to be an act of justice, warranted by the Constitution upon military necessity, I invoke the considerate judgment of mankind and the gracious favor of Almighty God.

In witness whereof, I have hereunto set my hand and caused the seal of the United States to be affixed.

Done at the City of Washington, this first day of January, in the year of our Lord one thousand eight hundred and sixty three, and of the Independence of the United States of America the eighty-seventh.

By the President: Abraham Lincoln
William H. Seward, Secretary of State.

The Constitution of the United States
Amendments XIII—XV

Amendment XIII
Proposed by Congress January 31, 1865;
Ratified December 6, 1865.

Note: A portion of Article IV, section 2, of the Constitution was superseded by Amendment XIII.

Section 1. Neither slavery nor involuntary servitude, except as a punishment for crime whereof the party shall have been duly convicted, shall exist within the United States, or any place subject to their jurisdiction.

Section 2. Congress shall have power to enforce this article by appropriate legislation.

Amendment XIV
Proposed by Congress June 13, 1866;
Ratified July 9, 1868.

Note: Article I, section 2, of the Constitution was modified by section 2 of Amendment XIV.

Section 1. All persons born or naturalized in the United States, and subject to the jurisdiction thereof, are citizens of the United States and of the State wherein they reside. No State shall make or enforce any law which shall abridge the privileges or immunities of citizens of the United States; nor shall any State deprive any person of life, liberty, or property, without due process of law; nor deny to any person within its jurisdiction the equal protection of the laws.

Section 2. Representatives shall be apportioned among the several States according to their respective numbers, counting the whole number of persons in each State, excluding Indians not taxed. But when the right to vote at any election for the choice of electors for President and Vice-President of the United States, Representatives in Congress, the Executive and Judicial officers of a State, or the members of the Legislature thereof, is denied to any of the male inhabitants of such State, (being twenty-one years of age,) and citizens of the United States, or in any way abridged, except for participation in rebellion, or other crime, the basis of representation therein shall be reduced in the proportion which the number of such male citizens shall bear to the whole number of male citizens twenty-one years of age in such State.

Section 3. No person shall be a Senator or Representative in Congress, or elector of President and Vice-President, or hold any office, civil or military, under the United States, or under any State, who, having previously taken an oath, as a member of Congress, or as an officer of the United States, or as a member of any State legislature, or as an executive or judicial officer of any State, to support the Constitution of the United States, shall have engaged in insurrection or rebellion against the same, or given aid or comfort

to the enemies thereof. But Congress may by a vote of two-thirds of each House, remove such disability.

Section 4. The validity of the public debt of the United States, authorized by law, including debts incurred for payment of pensions and bounties for services in suppressing insurrection or rebellion, shall not be questioned. But neither the United States nor any State shall assume or pay any debt or obligation incurred in aid of insurrection or rebellion against the United States, or any claim for the loss or emancipation of any slave; but all such debts, obligations and claims shall be held illegal and void.

Section 5. The Congress shall have power to enforce, by appropriate legislation, the provisions of this article.

Amendment XV
Proposed by Congress February 26, 1869; Ratified February 3, 1870.

Section 1. The right of citizens of the United States to vote shall not be denied or abridged by the United States or by any State on account of race, color, or previous condition of servitude—

Section 2. The Congress shall have power to enforce this article by appropriate legislation.

Index